BORN FREE FOUNDATION

Tiger
Rescue

True-Life
Stories

BORN FREE FOUNDATION

Tiger Rescue

True-Life Stories

Written by
Louisa Leaman

BARRON'S

Hello everyone,

I am sometimes asked if I have ever seen a tiger in the wild. When I say no, people seem surprised. But tigers are not animals of the plains, like lions. Their homes are in jungles and forests and, of course, they may have an inbuilt fear and suspicion of man.

I have seen a paw print or two and that was quite wonderful. I knew that here, in this particular forest, tigers were alive and well.

Big cats, of all kinds, have fascinated me for a long time. Going to Kenya fifty-three years ago, with my husband Bill Travers, to act in a film called *Born Free* (from the famous book by Joy Adamson), introduced us to lions—the story was about a beautiful lioness called Elsa.

When we started our animal charity many years later we saw all kinds of different wild creatures—but mainly in captivity. When we managed to rescue some of these from their cages or small pens, it was always a joyful experience. Our first tiger rescue, in 1987, was of six circus tigers. Their owner had no license so these magnificent animals had been confined in a beast wagon. The circus had been closed by Maidstone Borough Council who asked for our help. We managed to create a sanctuary for them in Bannerghatta National Park in India. Little did we know then that many years later we would be taking six more tigers to another sanctuary within the park.

It wasn't until the late 1990s that we were told about a little tiger cub in a cage in a pet shop in Barcelona.

This book will tell you his story—but one of the things that makes it so special is that the tiger, Roque, is still alive today! When he first arrived from Spain he went to live at the Big Cat Sanctuary in Kent where he joined five tigers that Born Free had rescued from an Italian circus.

We were then given permission to open a second tiger sanctuary in India, not far from the first. Only one of the original circus tigers, Greenwich, was still living and, when the new sanctuary was finished, he moved there in 2002 and was joined by Roque and the other tigers from Kent, as well as tiger Ginny from Limburgse Zoo in Belgium.

It is hard to describe one's feelings when you see animals begin a new life—a life so far removed from the circus beast wagon or the cage. It is wonderful to see them explore their new surroundings, enjoy their pools, hide in the undergrowth, relax in the sunshine, and hear the natural sounds of the bush.

Although, as you know, this book is about Roque, I wanted to mention the others we have helped as they are the "founders" of our tiger rescues and should never be forgotten.

They are just a handful of the magnificent animals exploited, caged, and denied freedom by those who care nothing about their real nature.

Roque is now 19 years old. He is an old tiger, but still handsome and healthy, and always remembers our big cat expert Tony Wiles, whom he met when he was rescued from the pet shop all those years ago.

In an ideal world no wild animal should be kept in captivity for our brief moment of interest. They are always wild, and it is in the wild that they should live, face their challenges, and fulfill their destinies.

A world without their footprints would be a tragic one indeed.

Virginia McKenna

Virginia McKenna OBE
Actress and Founder Trustee, Born Free Foundation

This is the real-life story of how a young tiger cub named Roque was given the chance of a new beginning, thanks to the effort and care provided by international wildlife charity the Born Free Foundation, and many others. Roque was rescued from a Spanish pet shop, where he was kept in a small glass aquarium. He now lives at Born Free's Tiger Sanctuary within Bannerghatta National Park in India. There he gets to experience a "real" tiger environment and be around others of his kind, like Masti, a disabled Bengal tiger, who lived at Bannerghatta with Roque for many years.

Roque

FACTFILE

- Male Sumatran tiger
- Birthday: May 17, 1998
- Rescued from a Spanish pet shop when he was five months old
- Favorite games—chase, hide and seek, hunter and hunted
- Personality—enthusiastic, playful, and friendly toward humans
- Grew more independent while at Born Free's Tiger Sanctuary in Bannerghatta, but always remembered his favorite caretaker, Tony Wiles

Masti

FACTFILE

- Disabled male Bengal tiger

- Wild-born, but unable to survive alone due to his front paw being mutilated in a poacher's snare, which meant his lower limb had to be amputated

- Personality—nervous and aggressive, but relaxed when close to other tigers

- Favorite activities—bathing in his water pool, batting basketballs around, exploring his specially adapted environment, and scent-marking his territory

- Lived at Born Free's Tiger Sanctuary in India for six years until his peaceful death in 2013

Chapter One
The Spanish Pet Shop

On the outskirts of the Spanish city of Barcelona, among the shadows of tall buildings and busy roads, a pet shop was opening up. Like all pet shops, it stocked a variety of animal equipment, including bedding for rabbits, squeaky toys for dogs, fish tanks, hutches, and seed feeders, as well as animals such as gerbils, guinea pigs, and rabbits. However, for a select set of customers, the shop also offered something a little more unusual. Behind the racks of dog leashes and flea collars, through a locked door and up a flight of stairs, there were two extra floors which housed a collection of rare, exotic animals.

he shop owner was pleased because he was
sell a very rare animal indeed: a tiger cub.
He'd sold many over the years, so he knew what a
good profit he could make. To him, it didn't matter
that the tiger trade was illegal or that tigers are an
endangered species, and he didn't seem to care about
the distress of the animals caused by the tiger trade.
As he watched the little cub cowering on the floor,
caged inside a dirty kennel, he smiled and thought
about all that he would be able to buy with the money
he would receive from the sale.

The cub, a small mass of orange and black-striped
fur with stubby ears, yellow eyes, and oversized paws,
gave a sad mewl. He didn't feel comfortable or safe in

FACT FILE

Less than 100 years ago, tigers were found throughout Asia, from Turkey to the Far East. Sadly, hunting and habitat loss have drastically reduced populations and today numbers have decreased from an estimated 100,000 to less than 4,000. The international tiger trade is illegal, but tragically continues, and today there are many more tigers held in captivity than exist in the wild.

such an unnatural environment. He wanted his mom. He wanted to be playing in the grass with his brothers and sisters. The only animals he had for company in the pet shop were a monkey, a raccoon, and a lynx— all kept in their own cages, facing uncertain destinies.

The cub was called Roque (pronounced "Rocky"), named after a Spanish saint. He'd been born five months earlier, in a Belgian zoo, but at three days old, still blind and suckling from his mother, he'd been taken and sold to the unscrupulous shop owner. This would have been a horribly traumatic experience for both Roque and his mother. Roque was transported across Europe, to the secret rooms above the Spanish pet shop, where he now cowered, frightened and alone. In the beginning the shop owner would have had to bottle feed him every three hours, to make up for the milk he could no longer get from his mother. At least he had a kennel now. At first, the shop owner had kept him on a shelf in a dirty glass aquarium, the kind usually used for fish or small reptiles—hardly a home for any animal, especially a tiger cub.

Over the years, the shop owner had illegally traded many different kinds of animals, including baby elephants, lions, leopards, and bears. Tigers were always popular—and lucrative. A cub could fetch at least $3,870 (£3,000) while a fully grown adult could bring in up to $38,730 (£30,000), which wasn't surprising, given what impressive animals they are.

Cubs were often bought by private collectors, who were keen on the idea of raising an exotic animal as a "pet." As soon as the cute little babies started to grow, however, the true difficulty—and danger—of keeping a tiger became evident. A full-size adult male with a voracious appetite, razor-sharp teeth, incredible strength, and claws that could kill a human with one swipe wasn't an easy or safe "pet." Sometimes the tigers were traded again, to zoos or circuses for a life of caged misery. More often, however, they were sold on and slaughtered for the Chinese medicine market.

Roque's next destination was anyone's guess.

FACT FILE

Tigers continue to be exploited in circuses, zoos, tiger farms, and as pets in peoples' homes. The demand for their skins as luxury rugs, their bones for "tiger tonic," and their body parts for other uses has led to increased killing of wild tigers. If more isn't done to protect them and their habitats, they could soon become extinct.

Chapter Two
The Rescue

Roque closed his eyes. There was nowhere to go, nothing to do. The four walls of the kennel were a prison. Meanwhile, the shop owner opened a tin of dog food. Dog food was not the ideal diet for a tiger, but it would have to do. He certainly didn't want the animal to starve. It had to look healthy if it was going to fetch the maximum price. Just then, the front door of the shop opened. The shop owner hurried downstairs, hoping that these were the special customers he'd been waiting for—a Dutch man and his wife—who'd been in the day before, talking about buying the tiger. The couple greeted the shop owner and immediately got down to business.

"Yes," they said, "we want the tiger."

"Come with me," said the shop owner.

He put a closed sign on the shop window, and then led the couple upstairs to the secret room. He didn't ask questions about who they were or what they planned to do with a tiger. Not his problem. As long as he made his money, the cub's future wasn't his concern. What he didn't know, however, was that these supposed customers weren't a married couple at all. They were actually an undercover investigator and a newspaper reporter. The undercover investigator had heard about tigers being sold as pets and had contacted the Born Free Foundation, who had in turn alerted the newspaper. The rescue of the tiger cub had been carefully planned. Not only would this investigation ensure Roque would go to a good home, it would provide proof that the pet shop was illegally trading endangered animals.

"Here he is," said the shop owner, nodding toward the cub.

Roque looked up and gave another pitiful mewl. He stared at the faces gazing back at him, not knowing whether they were kind or cruel.

"He was born in captivity, so the sale is perfectly legal," the shop owner lied. "He was only three days old when we took him from his mother, so the first thing he saw was humans. It's a good thing. It means he's tame. He'll make a great pet."

"Can we have his official documents, then?" the woman asked.

"No documents, but I'll let you take him anyway, for $3,870 (£3,000)."

In the wild, female tigers give birth to litters of two to six cubs, which they raise with little or no help from the male. Cubs learn to hunt and kill from around six months of age but remain dependent on their mother for at least 15 months, after which they will disperse to find their own territory.

FACT FILE

The couple calmly gave the shop owner the money. Roque huddled at the back of his transportation cage while a heavy blanket was placed over it to shield him from view. The sudden darkness was bewildering. What was happening now? The cage jiggled and swayed as it was carried downstairs and loaded into the shop owner's truck. Roque had no idea what was going on. He felt confused and scared.

The truck was driven to the hotel where the "couple" was staying so Roque could be transferred into the back of their estate car. The two vehicles backed up against each other. Both car trunks were opened. With haste, the cage was moved from one trunk to the other. That was it. The deal was done. Once the shop owner was off the scene, it was time for the rest of the plan to come together.

A team of animal experts from the Born Free Foundation was waiting in the hotel parking lot with a white van. The team included big cat expert Tony Wiles, veterinarian John Kenward, and animal caretaker Jane Livermore. As soon as they got the signal that

the tiger had been safely transferred into the couple's vehicle, they drove out of the hotel parking lot to the estate car and immediately transferred the tiger cub into their white van. They had to be careful. There was still a risk that the shop owner would realize he'd been set up. He might get aggressive and try to take Roque back again. The danger was far from over.

The team had to get Roque to safety fast. With no time to spare, they jumped into the van. Jane lifted the blanket off the cage, so that Roque could get some air—and his first glimpse of the people who would play a part in his new life, people who valued his welfare. Bleary eyed, Roque blinked and took in the four walls of the van. It was another confusing situation, with more unfamiliar humans—but at least they seemed to be smiling.

They rushed at full-speed out of Barcelona to a safe-house belonging to an animal-loving couple (friends of Born Free Founder Virginia McKenna), at the beach resort of Calafel. Roque was sneaked out of the van and into the house through the backyard. The team was careful not to draw too much attention to him—they didn't want people to start talking and spreading the word of his location. From now on, Born Free was going to be in charge of his care. But the undercover reporter's work wasn't over. She would write her story for the newspaper so that the pet shop's cruel, illegal animal trade would be exposed to the world.

Chapter Three

The Half-Way House

Roque's new home was a utility and shower room
in a basement guest annex. It was the only space in
the house that could safely contain him. Tony the big
cat expert helped as John the veterinarian carefully
tranquilized Roque, so that they could give him
a thorough health check. They clipped his claws,
carefully blunting them, so that he could be handled
safely. They also took this opportunity to put a collar
around his neck so that Roque could be taken outside
safely while his new temporary enclosure was being

constructed in the yard. Roque came around and quickly recovered. The overwhelming experience of the escape was now behind him and he was eager to explore his new surroundings. Tony attached a leash to his collar and led the cub outside. As soon as he was in the open air, he became energized and began to scamper about. His ears pricked up and his tiger senses sprang to life. It was clear he now felt more confident and was ready to play!

The next day, the team went straight to a DIY store to buy wire and wood, so that they could build Roque's new daytime enclosure in the yard, which would allow him fresh air and movement. It took a day for them to secure a fence of strong wire netting all around the courtyard. It was only a small area, but it was more space than Roque had ever had.

Tony started offering Roque toys to play with. Roque showed a keen interest in basketballs and melons, which he liked to bat around, smash, and chew. Tony had also brought a padded dog sleeve with him, designed to protect police dog handlers

while in training with their animals. He wore it under his jacket for the first handling of Roque, as the cub was quite excitable and sometimes tried to nip with his teeth. The sleeve enabled Tony to withstand the pressure of Roque's powerful jaws—a slight "nip" from even the smallest of tigers can cause a nasty injury. Roque loved the "rough and tumble" interaction. Finally he was able to play and behave like the young tiger that he was, rather than being stuck in a tiny cage.

Roque slept on a thick blanket in the shower room at night. Members of the team took turns sleeping nearby in the attached bedroom. This not only enabled them to keep an eye on him, but also helped them to bond with Roque. Despite the cruelty of his early life, Roque was clearly willing to forgive and trust kind humans. Tony, in particular, became a favorite companion. The pair formed a powerful connection. Tony, however, was always careful. Despite only being a cub, Roque frequently demonstrated his strength. On one occasion, he managed to tip Tony off a double bed, pulling down the mattress and getting caught up in the bedsheets in the process.

Tigers are renowned for their power and strength. They are capable of leaping long distances and can run fast over short distances, reaching speeds of up to 35 mph (55 kph). Adult male tigers can weigh up to 800 lbs (363 kg)—that's about the same as ten human 10-year-olds!

FACT FILE

The house in Calafel was only intended as a temporary home for Roque. After a month, the correct legal papers were ready, allowing Roque to be transferred to a permanent home at the Born Free supported Big Cat Sanctuary in Kent, England, where a special enclosure had been constructed for him. It was the start of a new, happier life for this little tiger, a life full of open spaces and friendly faces.

Chapter Four
Big Cat Sanctuary, Kent

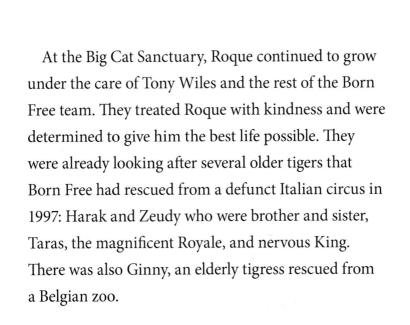

At the Big Cat Sanctuary, Roque continued to grow under the care of Tony Wiles and the rest of the Born Free team. They treated Roque with kindness and were determined to give him the best life possible. They were already looking after several older tigers that Born Free had rescued from a defunct Italian circus in 1997: Harak and Zeudy who were brother and sister, Taras, the magnificent Royale, and nervous King. There was also Ginny, an elderly tigress rescued from a Belgian zoo.

Roque immediately stood out, not just because he was young, but because he was a different subspecies. As a Sumatran tiger, from the steamy jungles of South East Asia, he would grow up to be much smaller and sleeker than the other tigers, with darker orange fur. The circus tigers were Siberian, and adapted to a colder climate, which meant they were bigger and bulkier, with thick, light orange fur.

FACT FILE

Tigers are divided into groups called subspecies. Today, there are five subspecies, named after the areas they inhabit: Bengal, South China, Indochinese, Sumatran, and Siberian (also known as "Amur"). Sadly, another three subspecies have become extinct: Caspian, Bali, and Javan. Each subspecies has developed characteristics suiting the conditions of their environment. For example, the Siberian tiger's large size, extra layer of fat, and thick fur help it to hunt and stay warm in the snowy Siberian winter. The small size and relatively dark color of the Sumatran tiger help it to hide and live secretively in dense, hot jungles.

Despite the drama of his rescue, Roque quickly adjusted to the new environment in Kent. After an initial quarantine period, he was able to explore a spacious outdoor enclosure. This was incredibly exciting to him, as he'd never had such freedom before. He rolled in the grass, scurried beneath bushes, sniffed the air, and chased fallen leaves. There was plenty to discover although, at first, there was also a lot to be cautious of. Stinging nettles and thunder had him rushing indoors!

Roque and Tony maintained their close bond. Roque would regularly approach the fence when he saw Tony coming, anxious to play, hopeful for a game of hide-and-seek or chase. He would happily allow Tony to stroke his ears and scratch his back through the fence.

The Siberian ex-circus tigers, by contrast, were very wary of humans. They'd learned to fear people after years of mistreatment. While the exact details of their life in the circus weren't known, it's likely they would have been punished to make them "behave," forced to perform, given limited exercise, and kept in tiny cages with no permanent access to water.

The female, Zeudy, and her brother, Harak, were in very poor condition. They struggled to maintain a healthy weight and Harak had a strange way of walking, as though his hindquarters were underdeveloped. Born Free suspected they had been closely inbred and would therefore never be as powerful or strong as normal Siberian tigers—which are regarded as the largest big cats in the world. The others (Royale, King, Taras, and Ginny) were getting

old and were also not the healthiest specimens of their kind. This didn't mean, however, that they were any less deserving of a great quality of life.

Roque, meanwhile, started to thrive in the Kent sanctuary. With an improved diet he grew fast and, within a few years, he matured into a fine young adult. He continued to enjoy seeing Tony, safely separated by the enclosure boundary, but it was clear he was a potentially dangerous animal. Tony tried to teach him to "play gently," but if he had his back to him, or if he stopped concentrating for a few seconds, Roque would instinctively pounce at the fence between them, almost as if he were hunting.

In the wild, tigers are "apex predators," which means they are at the top of the food chain. They are well designed to hunt big prey, with their short, heavily muscled forelimbs, large retractable claws, powerful jaws, and sharp scissor-like teeth. They are known as "ambush" hunters; they quietly stalk and circle their prey, before charging, leaping, and biting from behind.

With Roque's increasing size and appetite for adventure, it became obvious he needed a more challenging environment. The Kent sanctuary had been an ideal place to recover from the stress of his early life but the team was determined for him to live out his days in an environment that was closer to his natural habitat.

There were a few problems with the Kent sanctuary as a long-term home for Roque. For starters, the British climate was too cold. As a Sumatran tiger, Roque's natural environment was tropical heat. The low temperatures, cold winds, and regular rainfall of Kent were uncomfortable for him. The Kent enclosures were also limited in size. If Roque was to truly get in touch with his tiger instincts he needed space to roam. Sadly, the conditions of Roque's pre-rescue life meant he would be unlikely to survive on his own, so releasing him back into the wild wasn't an option. Thankfully, Born Free had a plan …

Chapter Five

A Passage to India

In 2002, the Born Free Foundation completed work on a new tiger sanctuary, set within a private area of Bannerghatta National Park, in the southern Indian state of Karnataka. It took two years to build, however the time spent was well worth it as it meant innocent tigers such as Roque and Zeudy would get their own patch of jungle and the chance to experience a life that was as close to "wild" as possible.

The Bannerghatta landscape, a mix of thick forest and shrubland, was already rich with wildlife, including elephants, leopards, bears, bison, deer, reptiles, and a variety of birds and insects. The main

park offered animal-spotting safari trips to tourists, but the tiger sanctuary was to be closed to visitors. This would give the animals peace, privacy, and respect, but they'd still have caretakers on hand to see to their food, drink, and medical needs.

In April 2002, it was time for the Kent tigers to move to their new home. For Born Free, it was an ambitious task. They were relocating not one, but six big cats to the other side of the world—sadly, Taras had died from cancer the previous December. The epic journey took two days and required a lot of planning and expertise.

The first step was coaxing the tigers out of their Kent enclosures and loading them into individual steel crates for transportation. Small pieces of fresh meat were offered as a reward to encourage them into the crates.

Curious Roque went in easily, but the ex-circus tigers were much more wary. The animal keepers had to work quickly and carefully, making sure that not only were the tigers safe, but that the keepers, themselves, were safe too. Even though the tigers were well-known to them, their unpredictable natures and immense power made them very dangerous. One mistake could be fatal.

The crates were then driven by truck to Heathrow airport, where they were placed in a quiet area while all the necessary customs documentation was completed. When the all clear was given, they were lifted into the cargo hold of a British Airways airplane and flown to

Chennai, accompanied by a team of veterinarians and animal keepers. During the nine-hour flight, the tigers were checked on frequently to make sure they weren't overly distressed or uncomfortable. When the plane finally landed, the tigers were given water in their crates, then placed on trucks and driven for another 11 hours to Bannerghatta.

Throughout the journey, Roque was quiet and subdued, perhaps unsettled by another confusing transportation experience. There is no doubt that such a long journey was a stressful experience for him and the other tigers, but they had endured worse hardships in their lives. And ultimately, although these tigers didn't know it yet, it was a journey to a better life.

Chapter Six

Bannerghatta

The Bannerghatta Tiger Sanctuary was divided into separate enclosures, known as "kraals." Roque and the circus tigers each had their own forest kraal, providing around a hectare of natural forest habitat and access to water. They also had a covered night enclosure. Indian law stated that all captive tigers should be kept inside at night, to protect them from poaching and other dangers. Born Free, however, wanted the tigers to be outside 24/7, to give them as natural a lifestyle as possible. They negotiated with the Indian authorities and it was agreed that the tigers could have special outdoor night kraals—grassy areas, near the caretakers' base.

Tony and the team were delighted by how quickly the tigers became accustomed to their enclosures. Roque, in particular, was very excited about his new forest home. At first, he stayed close to where he'd been released, under the watchful eye of the staff, but within a few days he started to get curious about his surroundings. Soon he was lounging in his pool, rolling in the grass, and enjoying the heat of the sunshine. Not surprisingly, he continued to seek attention from the Born Free caretakers. His life, so far, had been spent in their company, so their presence was familiar, and probably quite reassuring. He frequently rubbed himself against the enclosure fence to be stroked. Sometimes he pushed his ears against the wire, to see if someone would tickle them. His love of people was a charming sight, but the team also hoped that, in time, with the freedom of his forest kraal, he would become more independent and more like the tiger he was born to be.

Roque seemed more content here than in his previous homes, no doubt due to the increased space and his new-found independence. He was finally experiencing a life much closer to that enjoyed by his wild relatives. The one major difference was that he didn't have to hunt to eat. At the sanctuary, Roque and the other tigers were provided with all the food that they needed, including beef and chicken. No matter how deep in their forest kraals they hid, they always came out for feeding time. The caretakers paid careful attention to their condition, making sure they didn't lose or gain too much weight. Zeudy and Harak seemed to do better on a daily feeding routine, but

Roque coped fine being fed every three days, which was the pattern he'd be more likely to adopt in the wild.

With his energy and enthusiasm for life, Roque flourished in India. Zeudy and Harak, however, were frailer, a result of the abysmal living conditions of their early life. Despite their challenges, both Harak and Zeudy appeared to realize they were indeed powerful tigers. They seemed proud as they roamed their territory, and loved the excitement of the jungle and the deep pools.

Tigers are "feast or famine" feeders, meaning they'll eat a large amount, then not eat again until they feel hungry. They are carnivores— they only eat meat— and they mainly feed on large mammals such as deer, wild pigs, antelope, and buffalo. If the kill is large, they may drag the remains to a thicket and loosely bury it with leaves, then return to it later. When several tigers are present at a kill, the males will often wait for females and cubs to eat first, unlike lions, who do the opposite. Tigers rarely argue or fight over a kill—they simply wait their turn.

FACT FILE

The extremes of the weather in Bannerghatta provided many new experiences for Roque and the others. For much of the year, the park was hot and dry. The intense heat encouraged Roque to recline in the shade or seek refreshment in the pools. During these times, he tended to tire quickly and was quieter. It must have been a strange experience for him at first, given he'd mostly lived in the cooler climate of Britain.

When the monsoon rains came, the heat and dust were replaced with heavy downpours and cooler temperatures. At this time, Roque became more active, energized by the fresh weather. He explored and played and made full use of his large territory. The rains, however, also brought plant growth. Shrubs, bushes, and flowers came into bloom and trees blossomed. So, although Roque became more interesting to watch at this time, the rapid spread of vegetation made it difficult for him to be spotted!

The monsoons created other challenges too. When the rains became very heavy, Roque and the other tigers would become unsettled. They would take cover in their dens until the downpours eased. Another problem was the flying insects, which gathered during and after the downpours. Roque became particularly agitated by them. He would try to growl and bite at them, as though they made him grumpy. Eventually, he discovered he could escape these pests by hiding in the thick undergrowth, which meant sightings of him became even less common. This was a good thing though—it was clear Roque was starting to adopt more typical tiger behavior.

Chapter Seven
Tony's Visits

After a few months, Roque developed a knack of retreating deep into the undergrowth, burrowing into the tall bamboo, and only emerging at meal times. He patrolled his territory thoroughly and enjoyed investigating the variety of insects, lizards, and mammals that lived in the bushes. He also found a favorite spot beneath the shade of a bush, high up on a rocky bank, where he had a great view of the surrounding land. It must have felt incredible, having spent his early weeks in a glass tank on a shelf in a pet shop, to now have a vast stretch of Indian forest to watch over.

With his new-found freedom, Roque was less dependent on his caretakers for company, but his friendship with Tony remained. The Born Free Foundation continued to monitor their tigers, now so far away, and Tony made regular trips to Bannerghatta to oversee their welfare. Three times a year, he was able to see them enjoying their new life in the jungle, sometimes during the refreshing cool of the monsoon rains and other times during the fierce heat of the dry season. On each visit, he looked forward to spending special time with Roque, but always wondered whether Roque would one day forget him.

Each time, however, Roque was just as eager to see Tony as Tony was to see him. Clearly, he still remembered his old human friend and felt happy in his company. Even if he was deep in his forest kraal or high up on his favorite boulder, when Tony walked the perimeter, Roque would come running as soon as he spotted or heard him. They'd spend hours enjoying old games such as hunter and hunted, hide-and-seek, and chase—although Tony would stay on the other

side of the fence. Despite their closeness, Tony never took his safety for granted. He never forgot the fact that Roque was a powerful big cat with a potentially fatal bite.

If Roque was in a quieter mood, then sometimes they would just lie down beside each other, on either side of the enclosure fence, and watch the world go by. At other times, Roque would show off. He'd proudly go to the top of his territory and repeatedly get in and out of his large pool, then parade around for Tony to see—almost as if he wanted Tony to join him for a swim!

Unlike most members of the cat family, tigers are good swimmers and often cool off in lakes and streams during the heat of the day. They play in the water when young, and as adults, they can swim several miles (kilometers) to hunt or cross rivers. Some tigers have been known to swim almost 19 miles (30 km) in a day. That's nearly the distance from England to France!

The ex-circus tigers were less interested in interaction with humans. They preferred to be alone. Tony's time with them tended to be more about observing than playing. Zeudy, the Siberian female, would sometimes show interest and greet him, but would then retreat quickly.

On some of Tony's visits, during the rains, when the forest was very overgrown, a glimpse of striped black and orange fur was all the tiger he saw. He didn't mind though. He was delighted that all of the tigers, including Roque, were becoming "wilder," disappearing into the undergrowth, camouflaged by branches and bushes.

The distinctive striped coat of the tiger provides excellent camouflage among trees and tall grasses, helping them to sneak up on prey without being spotted. No two tigers have the same markings on their coats; they are as individual as human fingerprints. Just like housecats, the markings on a tiger's fur are also found on their skin, so even a shaved tiger would still show its stripes.

FACT FILE

Chapter Eight
Keeping the Tigers Busy

One of Tony's roles when visiting Bannerghatta was to make sure that the forest enclosures were being properly managed, so that they were safe and interesting for the tigers. As one of the younger tigers, Roque was the most energetic, but since he wasn't living fully "wild," and didn't have to use his impressive physical abilities to hunt for himself or chase off rivals, it was vital that he had enrichments in his kraal. These enrichments were crucial to challenge him, use up excess energy, and encourage his zest for life.

Like many tigers, Roque was fond of submerging himself in water. Water gave him a place to hide, play, cool off, or relax. It made him happy, so it was important that he had constant access to pools. In the dry season, if the monsoon rains had been poor, some of the natural pools in the forest enclosures would dry up completely. Luckily, there were also several man-made ones, which could be topped off from a water tank.

As well as providing water, the staff constructed a variety of climbing platforms between the trees, grew different shrubs and plants, and provided toys, to see if the tigers showed interest in them. When new activities were added, the tigers would watch curiously, and then try them. If they enjoyed what was offered, they'd use them repeatedly. Basketballs were always a favorite with Roque. Sometimes they were simply thrown into the enclosure for him to chase and grab. Other times they were hung from long poles, so he could jump up and bat them or attempt to pull them down—just like a domestic cat with a toy!

FACT FILE

Tigers are extremely agile and have flexible bodies designed for running, jumping, and climbing. Their senses are finely tuned. They have excellent eyesight uniquely adapted to seeing in the dark, acute hearing, and a good sense of smell. Their night vision is six times better than humans.

A large variety of trees and plants grew in the kraals, including bamboos and evergreens. After the rains, these plants could become very dense. Although the tigers probably enjoyed the privacy they provided, it also made it difficult for them to move around. Regular clearing was important. Cutting back the undergrowth also reduced the hazard of thorns and created more grassy spaces.

On one of Tony's visits, Roque was not himself. He seemed sad and quiet. It turned out he had a nasty injury caused by a thorn in the padded part of his paw. The thorn had been removed, but it had caused an unpleasant infection, which required treatment with antibiotic ointment. Luckily, due to his confidence around humans, Roque tolerated medical help very well. He sat patiently in his special treatment cage,

while one caretaker applied the ointment through the bars and another stroked his back and quietly reassured him. Pretty soon, he was up on his feet and happy to be scuttling away to his forest hideaway.

As time went by, some of the old ex-circus tigers were coming to the end of their lives. Even though death is a natural part of the cycle of life, losing a tiger always brought great sadness to the sanctuary. The Born Free Foundation, however, was grateful that these tigers had been able to escape the hardships of their early lives in captivity, and enjoy several years of happiness at the Kent and Bannerghatta sanctuaries.

Tigers can live for approximately 15 years in the wild and longer in captivity. Old and injured tigers have difficulty hunting fast-moving prey, and have been known to attack humans and domestic cattle, earning them their fearsome reputation. Tigers rely heavily on their powerful teeth for survival. In the wild, if they lose their canines (tearing teeth) through injury or old age, they can no longer kill and are likely to starve to death.

FACT FILE

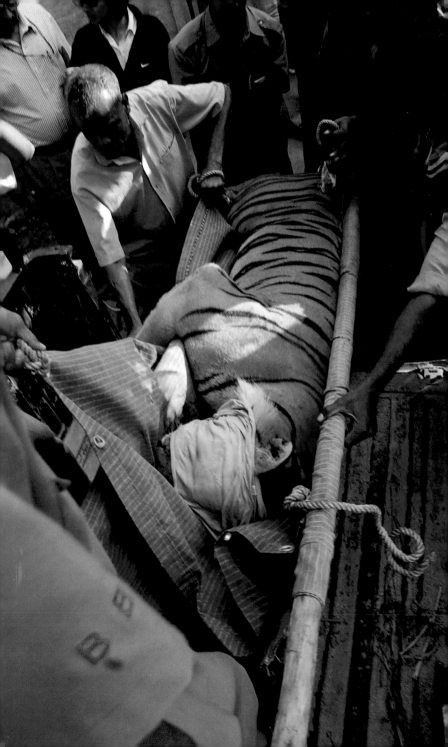

Chapter Nine

A "Wild" Newcomer

In 2007, a magnificent wild Bengal tiger named
Masti was introduced to the park. Masti was different
from the other tigers in several ways. First, he was an
indigenous Bengal tiger. Second, he was officially
"wild," unlike Roque, who'd been raised by humans
in captivity. As a Sumatran tiger, Roque had always
been of great interest to the Indian caretakers at
Bannerghatta, because he was much smaller and
sleeker than the Bengal tigers indigenous to India.
Now that they had a Bengal resident to compare him
with, the differences were even clearer.

FACT FILE

Bengal tigers are the most common of all tiger subspecies and the second largest after the Siberian tiger. Bengal tigers can weigh up to 500 lbs (227 kg). Due to their size, they have no natural predators in their native habitat— the only threat to their existence is humans. They live in the dense jungle and mangrove swamps of India, Nepal, Bhutan, and Bangladesh.

Masti (named after the Mastigudi road that was close to where he'd been found) had been living in Nagarahole National Park, a large tiger habitat in southern India, until one day he was caught in a poacher's trap. The trap, designed to catch wild boar, caused a massive injury to his left foreleg. He managed to pull his leg free and struggled to a nearby cave, which must have been a long and agonizing experience. He was captured by the authorities and taken to Mysore Zoo, but his injury was so severe he had to have the lower part of his front leg amputated.

Without a front paw, the veterinarians knew Masti's mobility would be restricted and that he would never be able to hunt again. Without being able to hunt, his chances of survival back in the wild were hopeless. After two years in Mysore Zoo, he was taken to the forestry rescue center in Bannerghatta. For two more years, he was kept in a small caged enclosure, as there was nowhere else for him to go. Thankfully, Born Free stepped in and provided Masti with the next best thing to his old life in the wild—a permanent home at the Born Free Tiger Sanctuary.

From the day Masti arrived, the caretakers noticed his temperament was very different to the captive-bred tigers already living with them. As soon as he was released into his enclosure, he started demonstrating fierce, furious behavior: growling, lashing out, and throwing his bodyweight around. His years of confinement had clearly been very frustrating for him and now he was unleashing his anger. He was highly aggressive toward humans, which wasn't surprising, given what they'd done to him. Staff had to strengthen the perimeter of his enclosure, since whenever they came near, he charged at the fence—and if a large Bengal tiger like Masti broke free, the consequences would be terrible.

Tigers hiss and growl when they are about to attack. They are known for their roar, but they do not normally roar to frighten other animals. The roar is used to communicate with other far-off tigers. A Bengal tiger's roar can carry for over 1.8 miles (3 km) at night.

FACT FILE

The Born Free Foundation realized Masti needed a spacious forest kraal, like the other tigers, where he could get away from the busy central area and find peace. The problem was, because of his disability, simply releasing him into the undergrowth might be dangerous for him as movement would be difficult and possibly hazardous. So, a special forest environment was created, with adaptations that would help him to move around more easily. Great care was taken in removing thorny shrubs and stones, which could cause pain if Masti stepped down heavily using his one front paw. Platforms were constructed that he could easily climb on, and interesting features such as logs and tires were added. And, since he was so comfortable with water, a large concrete water pool was made for him to relax in.

When the day came to release Masti into this new enclosure, everyone watched anxiously. They were delighted to see that from the moment Masti stepped inside his wild tiger senses returned to him. He began to react to every little sound and movement. He also began spraying the nearby bushes with his scent, marking his territory, and majestically proclaiming his rule.

FACT FILE

Tigers are known to "mark" their territory in an effort to warn off other tigers. Territory marking behavior includes scratching into trees with claws, spraying urine, and rubbing their scent on to trees and bushes. Tigers can tell the age, gender, and reproductive condition of other tigers by differences in the smell of urine markings!

For the first time since his captivity, Masti became utterly calm and sure of himself. Clearly, he was glad to be away from the prying eyes of the humans he'd understandably grown to loathe.

Masti's presence at Bannerghatta had an interesting effect on the other tigers living there. One of the remaining male Siberian tigers, Harak, suddenly took to sleeping at the fence near Masti's night kraal—unusual for a tiger who usually spent his time hidden away in the forest. At first, Tony and the caretakers wondered whether Harak was trying to strike up a friendship with Masti, but they suspected it was more likely he was being a typical tiger and trying to defend his territory from the newcomer. As time went on, however, no animosity developed between them. Perhaps they were being friendly after all? Or perhaps Harak was simply anxious to watch Masti and pick up a few tips on wild tiger habits?

So Bannerghatta now had three tiger subspecies living at the sanctuary: Sumatran, Bengal, and Siberian. The keepers were fascinated to observe the differences between them, especially the ways in which they responded to the activities placed in their enclosures. To their surprise, Masti was far more curious than any of the other tigers, even playful Roque. As soon as Masti spotted a new item, he would investigate it.

He loved balls and would bat them around his night enclosure for hours. He particularly liked knocking them into his pool and watching them disappear and then bob up again.

Roque, by contrast, tended to ignore new activities in his enclosure for a few days before investigating them. When he finally took an interest, he would explore thoroughly, and if he liked an item, he'd enjoy it over and over again. Ultimately, however, he was slower to respond to changes than Masti. Tony

couldn't help wondering whether a life in captivity had dulled Roque's natural tiger instincts. He had such a zest for life, and was certainly fond of games with humans, but when it came to being alert and aware of the forest environment, wild Masti, despite his disability, had the edge.

Chapter Ten
Roque's Future

Tony has continued to visit the Bannerghatta tigers for the Born Free Foundation. On every trip, he has made an effort to spend time with them, although this hasn't always been easy, especially during the rainy season when thick overgrowth makes it difficult to spot them in their forest enclosures. He was pleased that the staff at Bannerghatta worked hard to keep developing and improving the enclosures, so that the tigers were continuously challenged. The staff also did their best to keep the tigers as healthy as possible, adapting their diets and treating any infections or stomach problems quickly.

Even so, nature took its course and Ginny, the ex-zoo tiger, and the ex-circus tigers eventually died. Each of them had a respectful Indian cremation, then their ashes were scattered in the park.

FACT FILE

A tiger's bones and other parts are thought, in some cultures, to have healing properties. Indeed, throughout history, tigers have been associated with luck, magic, illusion, courage, stealth, and fertility. They have also been viewed as both forces of good and evil. This has led to an interest in using their body parts and products in rituals, for medicines, and as gifts. Unfortunately, this demand for tiger body parts and products leads to poaching of tigers in the wild.

After six years at Bannerghatta, Masti, the Bengal tiger with the ferocious growl, died in 2013. Shortly before Masti's death, Tony visited the sanctuary. Tony saw that Masti was sleeping a lot and looked weak, but comfortable. They estimated he was about 17 years old. Although famous for hating the presence of

humans, in his later years Masti became more tolerant of them, as though he'd finally accepted they were on his side and trying to help.

Roque became the only surviving tiger from the original six brought over from Kent. Now a mature adult male, living a much happier lifestyle than if he had been bought as a pet from the Spanish pet shop, he continues to flourish. He enjoys good health and his rich orange coat is always glossy.

A few years ago, Tony and Alison Hood, Born Free's Campaign Director at the time, traveled to Bannerghatta to visit Roque. Increasingly, it had been hard to see him, as he'd been spending more and more time being "wild" in the depths of his forest kraal, only returning to the central yard for a feed. On this occasion, however, staff had kept him in the yard, knowing there would be visitors.

Tony chatted with some of the staff, while Alison, anxious to say hello to the magnificent tiger, approached the fence. Noticing a new visitor, Roque pricked his ears. He started to approach, to offer his tiger greeting, then moments later, Tony appeared. Instantly, Roque changed course, ignoring Alison, and going straight to his old friend! It was clear he would never forget the man who helped raise him from a cub. Roque spent several minutes rubbing up against the fence near Tony, showing his affection. After that, he turned and walked back through the gate to his forest area, then disappeared from view.

To Tony, it was the best of both worlds. Roque still recognized and cherished a friendly human face, yet he also welcomed a life away from people, living deep in the forest, where a wild tiger should be.

Read all
the rescue
stories

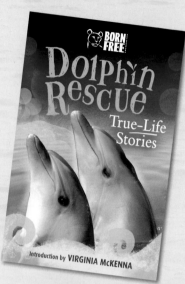

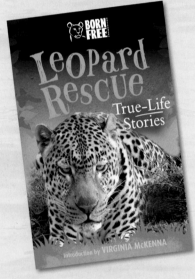

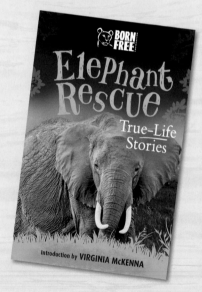

Keep Wildlife in the Wild

Go wild with Born Free

Welcome to the Born Free Foundation, where people get into animals and go wild! Our wildlife charity takes action all around the world to save lions, elephants, gorillas, tigers, chimps, dolphins, bears, wolves, and lots more.

If you're wild about animals, visit
www.bornfreeusa.org
To join our free kids' club, WildcreW, or adopt your own animal, visit
www.bornfree.org.uk

Keep Wildlife in the Wild